Requiem for the Orchard

AKRON SERIES IN POETRY

Requiem for the Orchard

Oliver de la Paz

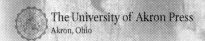 The University of Akron Press
Akron, Ohio

All rights reserved • First Edition 2010 • Manufactured in the United States of America. •
All inquiries and permission requests should be addressed to the Publisher, the University
of Akron Press, Akron, Ohio 44325-1703.

14   13   12   11   10   5   4   3   2   1

LIBRARY OF CONGRESS CATALOGING-IN-PUBLICATION DATA
de la Paz, Oliver, 1972–
   Requiem for the orchard / Oliver de la Paz. — 1st ed.
     p. cm. — (Akron series in poetry)
   ISBN 978-1-931968-77-5 (alk. paper) — ISBN 978-1-931968-74-4 (pbk. : alk. paper)
   I. Title.
   PS3554.E114R47 2010
   811'.6—dc22

2009043757

The paper used in this publication meets the minimum requirements of American
National Standard for Information Sciences—Permanence of Paper for Printed
Library Materials, ANSI Z39.48–1984. ∞

Cover: Detail from "Light II" by Andie deRoux. © 2010 Andie deRoux, licensed by
Grand Image, Ltd.

Requiem for the Orchard was designed and typeset by Amy Freels. The typeface,
StonePrint, was designed by Sumner Stone. The display type is Avenir.
Requiem for the Orchard was printed on sixty-pound natural and bound by
BookMasters of Ashland, Ohio.

Contents

Part II

For Meredith and for Lucas

In Defense of Small Towns

When I look at it, it's simple, really. I hated life there. September,
once filled with animal deaths and toughened hay. And the smells

of fall were boiled-down beets and potatoes
or the farmhands' breeches smeared with oil and diesel

as they rode into town, dusty and pissed. The radio station
split time between metal and Tejano, and the only action

happened on Friday nights where the high school football team
gave everyone a chance at forgiveness. The town left no room

for novelty or change. The sheriff knew everyone's son and despite that,
we'd cruise up and down the avenues, switching between

brake and gearshift. We'd fight and spit chew into Big Gulp cups
and have our hearts broken nightly. In that town I learned

to fire a shotgun at nine and wring a chicken's neck
with one hand by twirling the bird and whipping it straight like a towel.

But I loved the place once. Everything was blonde and cracked
and the irrigation ditches stretched to the end of the earth. You could

ride on a bicycle and see clearly the outline of every leaf
or catch on the streets each word of a neighbor's argument.

Nothing could happen there and if I willed it, the place would have me
slipping over its rocks into the river with the sugar plant's steam

or signing papers at a storefront army desk, buttoned up
with medallions and a crew cut, eyeing the next recruits.

If I've learned anything, it's that I could be anywhere,
staring at a hunk of asphalt or listening to the clap of billiard balls

against each other in a bar and hear my name. Indifference now?
Some. I shook loose, but that isn't the whole story. The fact is

I'm still in love. And when I wake up, I watch my son yawn,
and my mind turns his upswept hair into cornstalks

at the edge of a field. Stillness is an acre, and his body
idles, deep like heavy machinery. I want to take him back there,

to the small town of my youth and hold the book of wildflowers
open for him, and look. I want him to know the colors of horses,

to run with a cattail in his hand and watch as its seeds
fly weightless as though nothing mattered, as though

the little things we tell ourselves about our pasts stay there,
rising slightly and just out of reach.

Part I

Requiem

The hours there, the spindled limbs and husks

of dead insects. The powders and the unguent

smells. What's left, now, of the orchards?

What shape and hammer? What clang of apples?

What crease of brown paper sacks with greasy sandwiches?

What salt burned into the brim of my cap?

What spines? What limb-aches from paintbrush

handles? What white acrylics spattered on green

and dense humidity of dew from grass?

Where lies the fruit trees and the hardy stock?

Where lies the open acre where we broke bottles

with pellet guns during break? Where we shot

feral cats and rabbits? Where no animal was safe

from the ferocity of boy?

At the Time of My Birth

I wondered how long I could go on
once the rain had stopped. My nerves

were wedged like wings under a hat.
Corncobs bobbed in boiling water. I kept

a fist in my mouth. I was strident.
The neat house curved like a draining sink.

Hot cars shined outside. Their engines
snapped like a chamois. I never

wanted to leave. The streets were suet-thick.
The hucksters had tinny voices. They had

swollen drums. They had gravel underfoot
and tongues that could peel citrus.

Radios throbbed. The wet hush
of my breath flung itself to mother.

The soft dark skin. The sweet
curl of the arm. The hum.

Ablation as the Creation of Adam

The world is always beginning.
A face sweeps over in the vertigo of anesthesia.

A light gauze or a saline wash . . . something to ease me
into this century tells me about the first darkness.

In the beginning, there was a whole me. There was
an end I could not see. And there were sounds—a siren

set the hounds off. In between crickets, a radio.
And between the radio, the hush of a respirator.

The aurora of the surgical lamp formed blue rings
behind shut eyes. Let there be and there was . . . gossamer thin,

the numbed pulse. Pulse, the memory of the heart.
Heart, the now-tongue. The here-flower.

Useless is the thing taken out of the body. Little stinkweed.
Little broken thrush. What's left—a socket. A keyhole.

I used to have something to miss; now my neck's a rattletrap.
Thus my body was corrected. A hand moved the waters

and said flesh be done. And it was done. Evening.
Morning. The sterile tube shunted into my neck.

And it was good. I rose, fawn-weary. The stun of spiced cleaner
cooled the room. Nothing like the clean of a new world

with my new none-body. My "hardly notice."
A new clock is wound behind the curtain.

The cut is now a blush. Apoplectic ravine. Cave scrawl.
My zippered nest. Pink ellipsis, I shall name you, my flamingo.

Somewhere, birds rise above the African coast like blown tissue.
The volcanic sun silhouettes their wings as they lift off. Then, the dizzy horizon.

Self-Portrait as the Burning Plains
of Eastern Oregon

Let me start with fire. A little blaze lit to clear back the scrub brush
brought by the winter storms. Let the air ting with each leaf pop
as the ash of prairie grasses rise skyward.

And let that fire grow with each gust
shot straight out of the Cascades far to the west.
The curlicues of smoke fill a sky, void of mountains,

while the corralled horses several hundred yards away
pace nervously back and forth.
I'm trying to remember how everything settles down

after a fire. How the outcroppings of rock stand out farther
in those charred, moonish surfaces. I'm trying to remember
the nonchalance of a boy used to such things.

How the seasonal burnings turned the sky umber
and how each wind seemed to fill our houses with soot.
Springtime meant that everything would burn

and so I, too, would torch my name into every picnic bench,
every combustible. A book of matches and a boy was never
an accident. Nor was the little recourse I had in those days.

Boredom was an arrow shot straight into the ground. But I'm here now.
My name is not a fire. My name is not a story of fire.
I've got nothing in common with that element, save contempt

for the place of my youth and a hunger for air.
I'm watching the horses closely—how they're starting to canter
in circles as the heat from the brush blurs the atmosphere,

makes everything look like it's underwater.
There's beauty in their fear, like the stun of a hushed landscape
after a catastrophe. And there's beauty in a boy,

shameless in his need for moments to explode.
That hunger? If you hold your breath long enough, you can feel
the weight of the horses as they run in faster and faster circles

but really, they're in no mortal danger. They'll settle down
to a trot, then rub their sides against the fence posts to feel warmth.
Time takes air and fuel and in the end what's left is smoke.

A blacked-out soda can. Maybe a plastic lid fused to stone. A refusal
to forget childhood's scald. But also a kind of forgiveness. Really,
there's nowhere to run, save in ever-widening arcs.

In that broad expanse of charred land, the wind moves
without impediment like a boy grown used to his name. And what's left
of the brush crumbles to the touch.

Sticks and Stones

When I was a child, I was afraid of my name.
Tender, I was a shuddering tailfin:

shark-bit and gray. In order to purge fear
I'd recite my name until it sounded

of helicopter blades or ghosts. Oliver, Oliver, Oliver
soon morphed into ah! liver!

and other children soon became
harmoniously red in their jests

like the blur of a pinwheel. Sky-eyed,
I would endure octaves, decrees,

whole legions of stutters. How martyred was I
in my resignation? How wind-swept and pure?

The world was lush and androgynous. We were little
naked birds chirring into the others' ears, him to her.

One child, later, wanted to eat my name,
her mouth large and terrible. It rent, slow . . .

sinister, a split in the sails of a skiff doomed.
Dead in the water. Other children would resuscitate it

so that the name was constant as wind through canyons.
There were caves and there were caves.

Dangerous little fluids, we were trickling, then still
giving a pause to breathe. And again we would take up

these pellets and dash them against our ears
leaving depressions nudged enough to hold water.

I still don't know what resides at the back of one's mouth.
All of it is forgery: steel to stone and wood to bone.

Self-Portrait with a Spillway

I imagine at the bottom of the spillway, bones. Some child,
perhaps, peering too far over the railing's edge. Maybe even

some bauble like an amethyst ring with a faulty setting
or another land to wish on, full of eucalyptus and flesh.

The possibilities keep me here, perched at the lip of what must be
the end of the world. Dizzy, my heart full of sleep and trains,

the way time is measured in small towns—I am nowhere in my life
so I've driven to the reservoir to right the thrill of the ache in my head

and to clear my thoughts of Nothing, America. The water skiers are sparse,
cutting their patterns into the manmade lake. The still air, clipped

by an outboard motor's glissando. It is getting dark,
and the whirlpool eats itself, petal by petal—then the whole rose

into a blackened stem. The rocks I threw, long gone. This is a good place
for revision, I think. Something final could be here instead of bits of debris

hurtled into the void. Therefore, the inverse of this world must be full
of constellations, some pattern, delicate as a bouquet. Purgatories

are ribbons tied to the boughs of alders. My heart is a top, wild
with inertia and glossy paint. I have lived steadily with my eyes

set to one point on the horizon. Here now, the water takes its laps
around the basin. The water drags and drags, the current, a lie

repeating itself. I wish to be lied to. To feel the spray on my face.
I do not want to look up. I do not want to look.

The Poet at Ten

Sound inhabited me. Summers,
the insect chirr made the coming months

seem mechanized. I moved that way,
my ear propelling me forward,

distracted. Lights from the county fair
dangled little spirals, red puckers

with my eyes closed. The Ferris wheel,
unquestionably distant . . . rising syntax and falling.

Things compressed and bulged, quiet
little breathings against my chest.

Mosquito, mosquito, I would call,
enamored with my own blood

which was not darker than the other boys',
despite their own chitter. I was unsure

of their little nips as one unsure of a scar.
And all this, the schism of what my ear picked up

and what I felt: the voice of my mother
through the electric fan chopped into bits.

Requiem

What's left now? The dumb hours of early risings,

      the laying down of metal irrigation pipe. Hush-a-bye

of sprinkler heads. We'd cinch the joints up, thread to thread

      and we'd take dabs of stolen chewing tobacco. We'd tamp it

down into the pink edges of our cheeks as we'd launch

      dirt clods at each other and hum to the prop-plane's

low pass over tree line. Bell-sounds, the thwack of aluminum

      on rock kept time. And so did the horizon, browning

from pesticides. So did our skins, browning in the bare acres.

      We were keeping pace with a dying river, the water pressure,

weak with each new fitting. We were keeping pace with our shit job,

      how we each knew we were getting ripped off and how the filthy

dollars we'd wad into our pockets couldn't buy us a fuller river, time,

      or the deep meaning of zinc powder on chapped hands.

Self-Portrait with Taxidermy

In my anatomy studies, I expected
fetal pigs, the pink bodies flush
against plastic in a swirl of formaldehyde.

The lacquered workbenches of the lab
and the light from the fluorescents
made us all ghoulish with our tools.

I was ready to live with the smell,
to pin back the skin with the packet of pins
and the scalpels we were given.

Instead, the teacher pulled, from a refrigerator,
six pheasants he bagged
on a weekend excursion to the sage desert.

Our disappointment hung in our faces, but
we shucked it off. The smell of the body cavities
and blood was an interminable horizon.

A bucket of baking soda between us all,
we had to skin the things yet be gentle enough
to keep their skins intact. I settled in,

the dissection pans turned white from the powder
with drizzles of some unguent, something none of us
had ever witnessed. An occasional bead

clanged on my pan. My body was riddled
with buckshot. I wondered if I'd be able
to salvage even the idea of pheasant.

I, too, had killed a bird, a headshot
from several yards earlier in the year. The loon jerked
then folded like a napkin, its neck

sagging like stems from a cut flower.
No one saw me fire the gun, even though the shot
thundered long after. That late afternoon

I had felt volcanic. The clouds came and went,
everything sputtered . . . candle-sure,
the way the color of childhood was meant to be.

The body of a loon rippled some distance.
It would soon wash ashore. I was praying
the lake wouldn't forsake me, utterly.

And when its form rolled up the bank, I was quick
to bury it, lest my father know that I had played
with the rifle and in my play, I had broken.

There is so much that clings to us, the licking sound
of the lake, the glint of a scalpel catching the green
aurorae from the humming fixtures.

The susurrations of our compressed breathing
was boundless. We were awaiting some deliverance
from our gory task. The *V* of a rifle sight

dipped true into afternoon biology. Our knives
rose and fell, and we quickly scooped the white powder
into the wounds we made.

The pheasants were surely things that would call to us,
to choose us. For, one by one we are called
to make something ready. To give back form

and put everything back in its place.

How I Learned Quiet

Begin with slowness—the drag of a candle's flame

down to the guard, and the pump of blood into the heart

as it sinks in the rib cage. Everything was spectacle.

Mother pinched me for squirming. The timetables lied. The games

were un-winnable. The priest looked down upon me

and lo, I was a fidgeting thing. God was in the desert

feeding me cactus flowers and locusts. I sank

my cheek between my teeth and listened

to the helicopters above us. Someone coughed. Someone

held up their hands and let fabric slide down to his elbows.

Insomnia as Transfiguration

Because the night is a scattering of sounds—blunt
branches hurtling to the ground, a nest stir, a sigh
from someone beside me. Because I am awake
and know that I am not on fire. I am fine. It's August.

The scar on my neck, clarity—two curtains sewn.
A little door locked from the inside.

Nothing wants anything tonight. There are only stars
and the usual animals. Only the fallen apple's wine-red crush.

Rabbits hurtle through the dark. Little missiles.
Little fur blossoms hiding from owls. Nothing wants
to be in this galaxy anymore. Everything wants the afterlife.

Dear afterlife, my body is lopped off. My hands
are in the carport. My legs, in the river. My head, of course,
in the tree awaiting sunrise. It dreams it is the owl,
a dark-winged habit. Then, a rabbit's dash
to the apple, shining like nebulae. Then the owl
scissoring the air. The heart pumps its box of inks.

The river's auscultations keep pace
with my lungs. Blame the ear for its attention. Blame
the body for not wanting to let go, but once a thing moves
it can't help it. There is only instinct, that living "yes."

Cussing in the Playground

I was irreverent in my youth. Not a hair of mine
was trained on words I said. At the first red flare,

I'd hurl curses. They were bees spiraling out of me.
Sometimes I wanted to gather them in the playground

with my bare hands, I thought, much like guiding water
into a plastic bag. I was stung for my wretchedness frequently.

At times I was the hollow place between my clavicle
and my neck. Troublesome, I was uncomfortable with eye contact

because of their slant and so I became troublesome . . . often sidelong.
Little mastications dotted my ears, telling me to shut up. So I would

clamp shut my heathen mouth. There was nothing
to prove to God or otherwise. In the untimely event of my death,

I decided I would look up. And if there were a blemish
on my face my mouth won't falter.

Self-Portrait in My Mother's Shoes

What did I know of the pumps, the flats,
the high rises of arches pressed against my heel ball?
First, the bric-a-brac of the closet was a visual ache. It struck me
like a metronome tick. I was completing some pattern.

Then the last, late music, whirly-gigs of notes
strobed from the fairgrounds. The Ferris wheel
was the tallest thing in the valley. It was late in the summer,
and the fizz from the carnival soda made me sick.

Then the décor of the vanity, the tubes, the jumble
of creams, and the ricochet of light off
their plastic labels. In the mirror, I was all fishbone.
Limbs akimbo with my sunken chest and my feet

precarious, the digits crammed into the narrow tips
of my mother's red stilettos—why the hell
did she own a pair of those? Over the airwaves
Don Henley's "Boys of Summer" made the world

so replete. So obvious. There was nothing to do
except disguise my life as the next. After the fairgrounds
closed for the evenings, I could hear the carnies
snarl into the darkness on their borrowed Harleys.

That night, I hardly existed at all. The town was alive
with gypsies, smelling of tree roots, grease, and beer.
I was penciled, wobbling like a fawn, ridiculously shod.
I must have looked over my shoulder a dozen times

for fear of my parents arrival,
earlier than expected. I climbed, rung by rung,
the possibilities of what would happen, having committed
the worst of betrayals in my father's house.

So I eased out of those shoes, becoming here again.
How weightless I was, dizzy from sugar
and other people's lives blowing by. How oblivious,
makeshift, and blooming.

Requiem

What shape and what hammer held our breaths

    in the storehouse where the migrant workers hid their liquor?

Where holsters hung from coat hooks on the landowner's door

    and where we moped, still shining despite our growing declension?

Vapor-bloom of apples crushed against the forklift's tire

    cooked our senses, and we'd dare each other

to steal the pistols for quick target practice. We'd stack

    mealy cores on top of each other, then squint and pull the trigger

back and laugh as arms jerked from recoil.

    We'd pick off rabbits and birds, and though the owner knew

what we had done he'd drink black coffee with bourbon,

    laugh, and shake off the radio static with a wave. Later

in our houses, our hands would arc to the tender and luminous

    memory of firing a round and the twitch of a body's last kick.

Eschatology through a Confluence of Trees

The orchard owner paid us a buck per row to coat the trunks,
so, paintbrushes in hand, we crawled through thigh-high crabgrass
like amputees. We knelt at tree trunks,
slathering whitewash on bark, erasing the idea of tree.

I was young and delirious with cash in my Levi's. Summer
was a new stone worn down with my thumb, and I stumbled
through rows, drunk on insect-hum. The apples were ready,
and red trucks gathered fruit before the sun or ground claimed them.

We were warned to keep away from the roads while gears
clattered and swerved through the grids. The air was a hymnal
of machines and insects, and when the rows were painted,
we took wine from the master's table and went deeper

into the woods. The world was vinegar and cider. The world
was the shock of wasps, and wine passed from the mouth
of a bottle between boys. Time was a polished balloon.
Later that year, after the work was done,

we would catch a worker meet his lover in an open acre. His hand,
ruined from the jammed mouth of a harvester when he had tried to pry
a rock free. And now his right hand forms a "T"
like the wings of a plane or a flock of wild geese.

With his whole hand he touches the back of this woman's thigh, dark
like the perpendiculars I had bleached all summer. Down the length
of her, his hand strokes while the fingerless stump pushes
his body off the earth. The pulse of harvested apples thump

somewhere in a warehouse, and a ruined man makes love
while drunken boys hide in a grove. Time now
is no longer in flight. It's an alder, forked beside a clearing,
and you can hear it sway above two bodies, and the sky is iodine-colored.

The sky is ablaze with pulp and dust. If I came back
to that hairless cheek of land where a man
and woman said nothing with their mouths, where I earned
my first dollar, drank my first wine . . . where summer

said nothing about the end of days or the end of youth,
I would be still. I would be my blood flowing, and the blood
pooling in my knees as I crouched and watched them. And the apple trees,
their white paint, would outlast any blossom.

At the Time of My Young Adulthood

I was cleaned and forgiven. I was
given nothing except a key ring, a grommet,

something pliable with a fingernail. Out.
I was told to get out with only shoes

and hairs tucked. The sky
was unpinned. It was a stripped room

with the light, chopped by the blinds. Shut up,
said the radio. Dance, said the automobile.

The air was a-roar with tidal rises. And I knew.
Knew the footage. I could be there

tomorrow, or, I could feel my way
for blocks without the lights on.

Rabbits were in the hutch. There were fences
and the world was earlobed. Shimmery and soft,

the tapers dripped inside of me. Saucers waited
to be filled. The air—wasn't it crisp and white?

Wasn't it a pinprick? A peck on the foot?
A spasm? A cry?

Self-Portrait beside a Dead Chestnut Horse

I am seven and in a field facing a dead horse.
Flies pucker around its open eyes like black-green oil
and as I walk to it, they alight. You are reading
my comic book aloud behind me with one hand
extended, batting back long grasses.

The afternoon rains have stopped and the front
of your denim culottes are dark with water. You do not
look up until the breeze pushes the tang past.
I am here because of a dare: to stab the heart
of a dead horse before a witness.

The whole town is marooned to this act,
the handle of the deer knife taken from
my father's dresser, moist.
I squeeze it to wring the last of me
out of its sharpened tip.

Grasses, hills, birds, the metallic smells of earth—the dead
tongue of a horse, barely visible between
its slightly opened mouth—I know I have been asleep.
Do it, you say, pushing me with your full weight
so that I almost fall on the cadaver.

Do it or I'll tell everyone that Oliver's a girl. I see
the paleness of your ankles. Your freckled wrists.
I see your breasts, barely flickering out of your shirt
as you thrust your arms out, still too young for a bra.
I would not know you now, with your son

and your past neatly tucked into drawers,
settling easily into quiet hours.
We do not know how it is we are called, only
that we hear the beautiful sweep of wind through our hair.
We do not know how it is to burn the name of a horse

into the air while riding across an ever-narrowing pasture.
The chirr of redwing blackbirds
thins me out, and the creek nearby fills
the watering hole where the other horses
stand and regard us like a crowd come to witness

an act of divinity. Overhead,
I hold the knife above the dead horse's flank—
how the will shines in it, perfect, cruel, and without doubt.
How it mirrors our deathlessness and the break
in the dark and distant sky. How it catches,

in air, the angle of the great brown body,
soft on impact as if to cushion us as we fall off the world.

Self-Portrait with Schlitz, a Pickup, and the Snake River

To be honest, I did it for a girl. And wouldn't you
choke down bad beers with the varsity high school
running back and the all-star wideout for one glimpse
of a thigh, a blond braid, a smile unmercifully cast
from the cab of a Ford pickup truck? The year
was perfect from the first, and I was happy
to linger in the tall grasses along the banks
while the saviors of Ontario, Oregon, toasted each other
for brave fights and even braver indiscretions.

We were plunging headlong into autumn
and loving our fall. We were bastards and we were
pissed. In love with ourselves and in love
with the long hormonal surge, sharp as a clarion call.
I was full of average tragedies: the fouled test,
the one betrayal at homecoming. Nothing
went better than planned. Skinny, quite linear,
I rocked back on my heel, tipping the can
for the last ounce of elemental prowess.

The girl in the truck clicked in disapproval
at the boys reduced to tree-stumps, their shoulders
pressed against each other as they slept off
the case. Cursing her luck she killed the engine
and handed me the keys. Both of us knew
the dangers of drunken boys. So I took her home,
the one sober boy, smelling faintly of beer and the river,
slightly metallic like the firing of a gun.
And we knew with the surety of a hand on a belt

there'd be hell to pay in the morning.
The steam from the Ore-Ida factory stunk up August.
From the dash, I could see lippy clouds fold and unfold,
making the whole valley smell of tilled earth. The Snake
was low and fumes dangled from months of no rain.
The pickup was not mine and neither was the girl.
Neither was the time, which swung around the curve
of the steering wheel. The day-warmed asphalt curled beneath
the Ford's near-bald tires and I could feel

the girl crying. Her head back and off to one side,
the stars, muddy in the swath of factory steam, I felt
something like joy, something like running in sleep
on that silent drive. What was there to say
to her? To the drunken football captains?
To the town I'd leave because of my minor loves?
Leave it to youth to make joy out of nothing.
The river, hard at work, kept pace with the truck.
It was the only thing keeping pace.

By Addition

The streets glare back at the headlights as the unpeopled
city winds around my head like ribbon, and I had hoped
the bass from the other car didn't know any names or principles . . . that it
    could thaw
the built-up civilization out of its one collective dream—the voice of the drum
guns behind me rich in its violence, and the pavement wet with rain
shimmers with the speaker's thud, a sort of pulse like a fly
in a glass, its wing-flits rippling the water outward to the mouth,
and I could feel in my stomach the shift of gears as I accelerate to leave
the sound, and the moon out now, from behind clouds turns everything blue,
and the aquarium light tells a kind of truth—that I don't want
to slow the car to let the other driver pass, that all the new light from his
    high-beams
and mine would set the night on fire, that our breaths
were vapor, phosphor . . . our breaths were leaving our bodies
in waves, redundant and slow—

Highway Towns

It's easy enough that they're out of sight, that the one off-ramp
leads to the split-open country offering no chance at love.

And that the timber cut by a long line of sons
is not the now and now . . . that every crack in the pavement

pantomimes the chiseled twist of a dying town's center. I've known
the dead in towns like these. Here, in Fossil, Oregon,

there are two museums which house nothing but bones. Here,
bluegrass is played on the lawn of the courthouse

and the same banjo player's knuckled pluck twangs a song or two
about the high school's one lucky turn at athletic greatness. The Oregon plains

recede as I advance towards the sea. All the empty spaces never speak.
I can only imagine that Fossil like my own hometown has its own

half-built temples, its own statuary filled with likenesses of the war dead.
That the world there is too bright, bleached, wide with acreage

and the calcified bones of animals. And that the small houses
dotting the surroundings are full of framed pictures with faces

who've had their own chance at love, but not here. The road glows
sepulchral white and I can feel my car tires hum

along the grooves of the wash-boarded cement. Somewhere, I know,
there's someone ahead of me, leaving another small highway town. He's behind

the wheel passing the yellow dashes on the interstate
as the mid-afternoon heat makes apparitions dance on the horizon.

Last Days

Auto wax, mousse, and AC/DC made us somebody,
and we ascended Fourth Avenue to Angus Young's
jangled guitar, up the one street that headed out of town.
So much for subtlety. A quiet town needs its monarchs,
and we were crowned. My hair—god almighty—
was glorious, shifting with the speed gusts.
A sea of teenagers from the surrounding towns, Payette,
Nyssa, Parma, Vale, we were punks and we were lovely.

The sheen of the newly washed pickups traveled up the hill,
each with its own pomp, though the circumstances took us nowhere.
We'd stop in the parking lot of the mall,
which was too broke for major retail—it gave in to local merchants,
Mel's, Cosmic Connections, Ye Olde Carmel Candy Shoppe,
half a dozen stores with the shelf-life of milk.

The lot swelled with liquor and cigarette smoke,
and we waited for Johnnie Dominguez, whose love for Lonnie Maeda
could only be cliché, to pull down his suspenders,
leave his hat in the cab, and brawl with Ernesto Mendez. The fight
was our extravagance. We'd preen with our letter-jackets
emblazoned with pins, our stitched chevrons, tassels aplenty.
We knew it was coming because the halls of the high-school
hissed with pressurization. So when Johnnie, close-fisted,
pounded Ernie until his cheek was pitted with gravel
from where he fell, face down, we felt the valves rattle from release.

And we ran after the siren lights broke the cool, laminar orbits of our youth.
We gunned our engines and squealed back down Fourth,
careening on adrenaline and rock and roll. We were inertia, reflex.
We were the dumbest movie, pointless, given to hyperbole.

As we rounded back up the hill, we saw Johnnie
and Lonnie, lips, blouse, hand, thigh, a spasm of desperate love.
Ernie, speechless, leaning against the hood of a squad car.
All the young cruisers' faces like gas flames in the metallic
rebound of their cars. How flared we were, the chrome bumpers
mirroring our confidence, our quintessential delinquency. How allegro.
How clenched. The red and blue spirals were our regalia.
The evening, bruise-black at the edge of the hill.

Eschatology on Interstate 84 at 70 mph

The interstate is tarred and dirty. Road kill
streak by in their infinite suicides, pelt after pelt. Nowhere.

There is a nowhere inside all this—

the null station throbs through the speakers. Perhaps
I'm being abducted by aliens. Static.
Then evangelicals. Then static again. I am driving off
the edge of the world.

God of the none-station is to the far right of the dial.

And to the left . . .
to the left are miles of dry pavement and Ritz.

The wheel of cheese cut into quarters, a jagged little fat,
moistens the sandwich bag. I am saving my crackers
having not seen a respite nor any sign of a villa.

Cedars outside the car stink up the ether. If they only knew
they burn so quickly. The guardrail

holds the landscape together in a severe haze. Then the ghosts

of foxglove. Long tendrils jut without blooms.

Self-Portrait with a Car Crash

Half lazy, half drunk, I rose out of the silence
of my car. The gatehouse hadn't moved.
The lawn, hospital-clean, didn't unfold like a map.

There was nothing holy about me
or about a new license to drive and what boys
are driven to do. Long I stood.

My tongue felt around my mouth
for a new syllable to honor the tire marks
chiseled into the landscape.

Mailbox gone. The crickets latticing my breaths
assisted my guilt. I was the only witness
save chunks of sod and the undisturbed nightlife.

In church we had begun the rites to confirmation,
and I confess seeing no bronze door
opened for my ascension. The priest was tired of us

because we professed to no understanding of obligation
save that we were obliged to meet for an hour.
I'm sure I was thinking of time as I inspected the fender.

The tires made little chevrons that crossed
into what was once a well-groomed yard.
I forced a prayer, compressed to ten minutes,

to the patron saint of desperate situations,
St. Thaddeus, wielder of the halberd, instrument of his death.
Briefly, I wondered if prayer was wise

given the lateness of the hour and the possibilities
of the homeowner returning to see my faults.
The car engine, idling, ticked with heat.

My once praying hands were again heavy at the wheel.
The landscape would be keeper of my absence.
Yet the asphalt would lie, would grant me

a few more shadows, the time-numbing road,
a moment with the top forty radio,
and that which was broken, unanswered.

Requiem

What crease of brown paper sacks? What amplitudes, our hunger

to be men? What cheese sandwiches and noon times

sick from soda and too hard running? Our hands were

the real language, and we hit each other with closed fists

just to unhinge the details. This was a nowhere place.

Miserable lunches and shit pay left us scuffling between

rows playing the tripping game or slapping down hard

on each other's backs, leaving red palm-shaped welts.

We were fuses, amped on caffeine and the urgency of youth—

and the orchard was hallowed ground. Like everything

we did was righteous and holy. Where the void was

nowhere and everywhere and where our brown skins, dappled

with paint and insect bites, were as pastoral as the understory

which held all things in its cold radiance.

No One Sleeps through the Night

Now the neighbor's horse is tied to the hitching post and the bats
keep their own vigils, but they are no ones. The no ones are

taking apart fiberglass in the attic. I hear them
at this hour in the wall. Can't you? The no ones are nesting.

It is beginning to drizzle. Can't you hear raindrops off the wet-dark cedars?
The toads are no ones too, licking their eyeballs

unafraid. They scatter into the green green grass
while the river shudders all awake. Little singer.

Little mouth. Tiny thumb. No owls are out. It is quiet
and the bed is a dark smiling place. The no ones are free

to come and go as they please. Ease back. Be the barest
duckling feather falling, falling. Fall. Carry nothing.

Little no one, peace and go.
I'll be watching while the sleep gods

lean and cast their shadows here. They bless the no ones—
caress them beyond the pull of gravity or grace.

And no one sings. Nobody is opening the gate
or driving the car. Night—all night my love,

windows return back our glances. Fiddlehead
ferns are on watch, thrusting their hands up

through the porch to hold the house down. The cat
is back asleep. Child, you are my moon apple.

My highly prized coin. Your bright eyes
leave blue glance tracks. Who are you? Geranium,

geranium, the balcony waits our paces rail to rail.
Little rabbit. Little mole. Little nuthatch, you blur me

into middle age. I feel old as stars, though the constellations
are unvisitable. And even if they were there are no

bread crumbs on the contrails. Lie down. Lie down. I'm lost.
There are only so many hours . . . only so much animal light.

Part II

Autumn Scene as Lullaby

In my nighttime, everything that moves loves
and is afraid—the white tufts of the hares veering
from the patchwork lattice in the garden,

your mother's incidental kiss on your lips,
the moon, the rooks, the tires on the bluing roads
to where the hellions in the rail yard adapt

their pitches to the winds and sidearm
rocks at the passing grain-cars in the dark.
They cheer the spark of the stones

against their speeding metal.
And in the absence of the trains, the world
returns to the heavenly bodies, the cold

dependable light of childhood. Son,
I have closed the windows letting moths
fight for all I have custody over—the lamps,

the books—cities of my own making.
Alder leaves fall and rise with the breezes,
and the train sounds like a witness from a past century.

I would kill for you. I would be killed for you.
Despite all the pathos love's door invites, the purpose
of nights like these is to ask the questions

and fail to understand. To listen intently to the trains
hurtling past all promise. To know
there are mysteries more merciful than the dark.

How I Learned Bliss

I spied everything. The North Dakota license,

the "Baby on Board" signs, dead raccoons, and deer carcasses.

The Garfields clinging to car windows—the musky traces of old coffee.

I was single-minded in the buzz saw tour I took through

the flatlands of the country to get home. I just wanted to get there.

Never mind the antecedent. I had lost stations miles ago

and was living on cassettes and caffeine. Ahead, brushstrokes

of smoke from annual fires. Only ahead to the last days of summer

and to the dying theme of youth. How pitch-perfect

the tire-on-shoulder sound was to mask the hiss of the tape deck ribbons.

Everything. Perfect. As Wyoming collapses over the car

like a wave. And then another mile marker. Another.

How can I say this more clearly? It was like opening a heavy book,

letting the pages feather themselves and finding a dried flower.

Self-Portrait on Good Friday as an Altar Boy

What I took to be God lit the dark between pews. We were all
humorless, huddled under the first stained glass station of the cross.
The candle flames pulled wick to wax, and I floated in my altar boy gown
as one afflicted with tongues. I could not speak, the collar flat
against my Adam's apple. The gray light filtered blue through glass
but held no meaning for me. I kept my eyes forward on the priest,
who looked holy with his arms outstretched, the sleeves of his robe
covering age spots I had seen earlier in the sanctuary.

This was the year of the long winter, and snow still hazarded
the pathways. I was contrite, tired of the flat whiteness of everything.
Junior high was a monument on a hill, light years from where I knelt
a stoop below the priest. I, too, raised my arms, holding the red book
up so he could read, his voice booming over my head.
This was the time of the long word. Sermons lasted forever.
The world was dark with the smell of salt on sidewalks,
and the sky from the doorway showed clouds, heavy and on the move.

I needed a destination. Somewhere to go where the biggest story
was a room whose brickworks could hold me like theater or TV.
But instead I learned need is the one allowed good, that grace
was chimerical, and that time did not listen during the story of mercy.
The musk of incense hung in the air before descending to the carpet.
At each place, I clanged the chain on the urn emanating smoke.
Everything in the church was too fragrant to be forgotten.
Here, the station of the betrayal. And here, Simon carries the cross.

Long we marched our way to Calvary. The afternoon,
as thick as a rind. Each section seemed the same. Our paces
were predictable . . . the trick, to make the recitations seem Orphic,
to stand and kneel with the passion of the saints in the statuary. To be
unflinching long enough for the pinks to sprout from the still-hard ground.
It wasn't easy and we were tired. My sugared brain hovered somewhere
just above the vaulted roof. The saints, surely, were never children,
and the hour curved like the road to the next life.

So many stations, so many porches with lights to hide
someone's absence. My knees grew tired from kneeling, and the weight
of the bronze smudge pot tensed my shoulder. The afternoon cars
dragged their trajectories through the air, and the interregnum
between prayers could fill a bucket with tacks. If only I could be
ecstatic. If only eternity were a short distance across a meadow.
I would go on, genuflecting before each alcove. Each pane
quivering at the lead seams with every gust of wind.

Once, Love, I Broke a Window

with a quarter fired from a slingshot to hear it
whistle. I ran as the glass cut the stillness of the room.

I regret my need to know what happened
to the coin that shook the house

with an unseasonable thunder, shook me
with it, my face burning as I fled. Once

then, a crow or the oiled shadow of a crow
found me and rounded the garden in dark crosses.

He fanned my body. The air was clean
except the bird's opulent throat.

Tonight I rise above the arcs of the crow
to your hair and the dark water of it

pooled on the sheets. The systole and diastole—
the arrhythmic music can't keep pace

with the past's nameless paperwork. I'm telling you
just this. A boy's missile passes

so violently through the heart. There is little
or no philosophy to this act. The window

shatters and the ears follow
the glass's most passionate telling. Let's say

you were there to stop the boy. Maybe
the games we play suggests our futures. Where

every fragment is the remainder of a childhood.
Where a crow is the soul of a lost quarter,

and where every confession, Dearest,
is a shard falling to the floor.

Meditation with Smoke and Flowers

It is Monday and I am not thinking of myself. My son, asleep
in his stroller, the dark conifers holding nothing but their scent.

I'm walking him to the place where loggers have cleared thirty acres,
leaving only ash and stripped tree limbs. The light now comes

to the places once dark—and now wildflowers where once
the moss grew thick and complete. The flame of something around the corner

and I'm thinking of the wild tiger lilies that line this gravel road below my house,
how they clump together, their stems bent down from the weight

of their flowers. How mouth-like they are, and how
their speechlessness makes the road quieter. Each flower is a surprise,

like the flaming tip of cigarettes in the dark. I think that the road
cannot contain all these mouths, though there are mythologies held

in check by the tongue. Like the story my father told me
about his father in wartime, and how his own father forced him, with the threat

of a beating, to go under the house for a cigarette from a Japanese foot soldier
bunkered down. I can see my father's small trembling hand,

outstretched to this man whose face is mud-caked, smelling
slightly of fire and lubricant for his rifle. The smoke from the soldier's own

cigarette takes the shape of the underside of the house, and I imagine
my father can hear his own father above him pacing.

But this road now is free of smoke. The logging trucks have taken off
for the night, and the tree remnants have smoldered into nothing

but charcoal. The wreck of everything is a vacuum, so too the wreck of a village
after war or the floor boards above a son's head in fear of his own father.

Here, though, there is nothing to fear. The wheels of the stroller on gravel
is the only sound, and the idleness of the excavation trucks harkens to

someone asleep in the uneasy dark. No, I am not thinking
of myself. I'm thinking of an agreement my father must have made

with himself years ago when the houses were burning
into bright bouquets in the nighttime. How, perhaps,

he swore he would not beat his own son while somewhere
in the afterlife his own father smokes and paces. Perhaps

there are no flowers in that place. Perhaps the lone soldier,
through with hiding, crawled out after the guns had stopped

and dusted himself off, the sun striking his face with its unreasonable light.
I'm thinking of my son, asleep, and of the wild tiger lilies. How frail they are

in the new light. Why they come. Why they spring up, unannounced
as suddenly as the promises we make with ourselves when we are young.

Requiem

And what salt? What hard cake on the hat brims? Our sweat

    gummed up the works, made us thick and slow-witted

in the early summer haze as we moped and stooped, painting

    row upon row of spindly trees, from the full-leafed

to the saplings. Our arms were heavy and our hands

    ached from carrying the gallon paint cans. We'd spill

a little here and there to lighten our steps. Moving was such

    theater. Acres blazed in the late afternoon.

Chemicals dusted our caps and mixed with our body mineral—

    white crystals and yellow film. We'd cough into our sleeves

and drink well water from our thermoses. And we'd pour

    the rest of it into our caps, letting it run down

our lengths, letting it mix with the mud, oil, and dust of ourselves,

    cold, decisive, and purely from the earth.

Self-Portrait Descending
Slowly into the Atlantic Ocean

There, just in front of the jetty, a boy had drowned
after a boat wake sucked him down. I know him.
To understand, to remember his name places me
among the several damned. It is of the best days.

The earth, fresh. The surfers practice
their cursives on the waves. That part of the beach
is cordoned off by yellow caution streamers
that click in the wind. Kids fly their kites by the scene,

while parents beckon them back to their proper blankets.
I am becalmed. The ocean pools around me
crossing itself back into itself. I, too, am
a boy and therefore, a camera—the glittering

sun-sea continuum is all I know of the world.
But it is not the world, and this shoal
has its share of ghosts. Each curl
comes forth to wash me, clavicle to femur,

my elbow tucked under my hand
as I hold my arm tight to my body. Stick
straight, I withstand each buffet, spray
on my lips and the cold fastidious fingers

of ocean water down my length.
Sand, like a thin mustard plaster on my back,
I shred the grains as I move. A scatter-fire of selves
leap into the water. I am trying my best

to wade to the boats, but the white
intensity of the sun holds me. Beneath me
does not look like the grave of anybody,
anybody at all. It is just green and loll. The diatoms

join and part and join again.
The gulls skirl above my head, sacramental
and in crescendo. They speak for my voice
because things are as they are. Slim islands

rise, just within my view, and I imagine
the dead boy is there, reigning over a procession
of candles and crosses. His ankles
festooned with peonies and he is forever

twelve. I want to talk to that boy. I want to hold
his hand and walk headlong to the horizon.
I want the masts of the tall ships to not be
funerary wands but kindling branches

held aloft to steer us from the depths
of these deep seas. Let the blood in my body
drag me down awhile. Let the coral
and the moray eel open pathways for us in the reef.

Let me remember a boy who was a boy.

At the Time of My Death

A horse will stray into an interstate. A child
on a tricycle will circle the block.

There will be lights. There will be a sound
from the television like a cannonball fired

into a lake. There will be fish and the sheen
of fish flung far into the sky who'll then

descend back into the lake like a hail of daggers.
There will be a pain like the cry of a caught bird.

A man will sit. A man will come to. Some
restitution will occur in a back room

atop stacked pallets. There will be violins
and gunfire. There will be mariachi,

disco balls, and laburnum.
Farewell, then, to the tortoise, the nipple,

and to the watch. Farewell to the desert,
Zen, and to ballet. All I want is a coin

for my tongue, a tomb for my body,
a mirror for my breath, and a shovel

for my memory. All I want is to know
what will become of the horse. Who

will catch it? Will it run? Will it veer?

Instead, I'm Here to Tell You Very Softly

I wished you saw it—the festival
lined our streets with white banners and if I seem
lost it's because the city held me
ransom and there were young girls
with baskets on every corner with tulips making
appeals for no rain, for the chalk paintings
on the sidewalks to not stream, to not muddy
or blur like the ruin of a New Year's party,
but the colors were everywhere, filling our sewers
and the sewers turned very beautiful with that
brought-in-from-the-ocean feeling you get
from nets full of fish, and yes, I wanted to eat
the hues but they were so quickly to the sea,
and yes, the white banners
sagged on the lampposts, and all the chalk art
was lost, sluiced, but softly, I'm here
to say that it's summer again and the undulant rows
of banners break my heart every time, every time
because when I tell you this you look so
kindred, so swift, so uncaught.

How I Learned the Obvious

The hand consists of the palm, four fingers,

and a thumb. But where I have trouble

is when I see the lines on your hand,

small things like rivers in dreams where birds

flying overhead lengthen and constrict.

I have trouble when it comes down

to your hand and the tributaries

faintly showing . . . the crumbling bits of loam.

Tall bearded men at the shore stand in white

robes with their arms crossed to pray.

The daylight through our window deepens

these rivers. The birds, which are white now,

take the place of the holy men at river edge.

Your hand closing fuses the two.

Morning is clear and sweet. It is a heaven

that I cannot fathom though it is obvious.

Requiem

What spines and what handles? The thin stripes of paint

    dried to bone on the boughs. The arc of our backs

curved. We were fingers bent on triggers—giddy

    and the trees would break beneath our savagery.

What we didn't kill, we'd break. Whole afternoons of breaking

    left us breathless and wet. The sweet tang of chewing tobacco

curled into our lips and we'd press the stuff and spit

    brown gobs at each other, until we were sick from the chase.

The bee boxes at the edge of the orchard were home

    to our dares, and we'd bet tins of chew on who'd do

the most damage with baseball bat to a bee box while suffering the fewest stings.

    It was stupid and we knew it. And despite all discretion, we charged,

our lips stinging from cinnamon while the open air

    hummed, impossible and kinetic.

Television as a Tool for Remission

It is like that. The night drinks its torches. The stars,
strange with the incoming clouds—a tattered fringe.

I'm snared on a celestial hook. The moment is zero
with the television untying some lace bodice.

A man in Paris is drinking port the color of a sports car.
He is a song of another century, and the bricks are biblical

in their age. Something will happen. A gun will fire,
a car will crash, he will make love with the vigor of an air raid.

Such are the possibilities of his life—paper will be cleaved
by scissors, a finger will tug a pink slip, a heart will be weighted on a scale.

Meanwhile, the reverse of the screen is the eye. Sometimes I play my trump.
Sometimes Jupiter comes out and makes holy the details of the evening.

The remote control is my enemy, my demon telescope. In this life
my attention is at the tender edge. Paper, dear paper . . .

dumb and delectable without a thingamabob to do. A poet's only espionage
is to pilfer the reliquary of the tongue . . . there is no gadget

hidden in the pen. No laser tucked in the spine of the book. James,
I have already forgotten this world because my brain's pisswater

and the details of my life are residuals of some god's nubbin.
I have forgotten my body because it is brother to the clock.

And because I am detoured, I say to you, go. Beware.
Promise you will not die. Promise to see where this world goes.

How You Came About in the World
Bewilders Me as a Cherry Tree Flowering

In the beginning there was
the dark of an empty box
and a hum of static
you can sleep to.

Wasps defended
the vespiary above
the picnic table, now
dust. Everything

was humorless and gray.
Empty cups lined
our cupboards.
Garages smelled
dull, like old oil.

I wanted to walk out

but there is nowhere to go.
Not even the straight
roads to town could take me
past the rubble.

Therefore, you were
a river of ribbons and
confetti from a piñata—
as if suddenly when I stood
to look out the window,
sunlight hit the tree and
it blossomed.

If, Given

If given a horse, a palomino, I'd ride
the high dunes to meet you at sunrise.

If there were no horse, only shoes and sand, I'd start
with the left foot, and with the right

I'd drag a path for you to follow.
The yellow storms would not pursue because

the law between us is holy. If there was water
and no desert, I'd sail for each celestial cluster

perched in the spiritus nebulae—
the planetary bodies, blemishes

of your skin. And if there were no compass,
I'd steer by shadow. I'd light a kerosene soaked arrow

and fire into the sky. I'd watch the parabola of flame
defy the worldly dark in the tongue of what must be

the end of paradise. And if there were no paradise,
then I'd be the horse. I'd bolt

as though the stables were on fire and you,
you would hold the bridle . . . you would ride.

Self-Portrait as a Small Town

Half in the street and half on the sidewalk,
I'm barefoot and bored with television, daytime
soaps and docudramas too blunted for me.

I want action, and what quickens my heart
are locomotives near the hardware store. I dream
myself into a train. I'd have a deep black steam

engine tuned to set my wheels dancing and I'd chug
beyond the warehouses with pallets filled with onions
stacked from the floor to the sky.

But August is no train . . . there is only
here and me and the meanwhile that makes
weeds along the railroad ties ultimately

important. Malaise, that untapped nerve
seeks a razor to cut the root growth, so
I pick fights with boys in the bowling alley,

and we practice bruising each other until the game
wears thin. Harmless, the blood in my mouth
from an afternoon's slow entanglements. After,

with bags of chips and 32-ounce sodas I spend a quarter
on a game and wait for the other boys' fathers
to pick them up, going from one mundane procession to another.

Always, this—an army of empty duties moving us
from one hour to the next. The sun bleaches the ground,
and a low plane draws an *X* over my body.

There is no train to come from out the shadows,
nothing in the dark coming to spare me or deliver me
past the threshold of my door. There will be

no television show for here, glamorously, breathlessly
bright and divine. The dullness, the expanse—
it's just the wrong side of the moment and I'm in it.

I walk the major road flanked by a greasy spoon and a bank
only to see the sky and a single car pass. A stray dog
trots across, toward the one grocery store.

I think, now I am nowhere and that my friends
are the sharp blue borders of window panes, and in every
house, families call each other by secret names.

That the open spaces will turn a young boy's stomach
inside-out, and that the lots filled with grasshoppers
could scissor me out of summer's bright face.

Autumn Songs in Four Variations

Stellar's Jays

There's one of them, beak upright,
and crown black as a demon's eye.

There's another on the branch above, a lookout.

He's singing to her as the forked alders
sway like sea grass. Meanwhile

the birds barely settle, their blue wings

rising this way and that for balance.
It is November, love, and the jays are hungry.

Winds have knocked over the feeders

and I've stopped setting out suet but still they come—
like little nudges, little threads tied to my thumb.

Soon the mountain passes will fill with snow

and my diligence with the seed will matter
just as these hours with you matter.

How can I keep you safe, knowing

each wayward tree could fall?
Where each evening's breeze rattles the panes?

Where a Stellar's Jay calling to the horizon means everything?

The Scarf of Maria Callas

Your night lullabies are the songs
of Callas from my youth.

She was beautiful and nearly blind.

Fall in the city was dangerous, but I still wandered
to clear my head past the bums picking up spent butts

and fingering the mouths of wine bottles.

The pavement stuck to my shoes, and trash
stopped up the gutters. I'd pause awhile

near the alley of a restaurant where I'd hear

her albums spin nightly. She'd be singing
Rossini operas as the busboys

clattered the dishes into the steam washer.

You should have seen the housecats
from the neighboring apartments clustering in that back alley,

swishing their tails as they waited to lick the plates

clean while Callas sang. They'd mewl
over leftovers in time to each note.

Then the crescendo of the orchestra

would drown out the city, and I imagined
Callas on stage, draped by an orange scarf,

her eyes on some familiar ghost.

Systole

And my recurring dream? It's sepia-toned
of my first night as a paramedic—my first call.

The spiraling lights of our ambulance made the man,

dying, look ghoulish, like a funhouse clown.
I couldn't bear to look at his face as the chest compressions

made him jerk like an inflatable cushion

while the engine's idling motor kept time with us.
It was a kind of song and dance, my hands on his ribcage

and the deep breath from the Ambu bag into his,

whistling back into my face with each push.
The way you're breathing now in your sleep.

Reprise: A Prayer for What Remains to Be Said

The maples are slightly green, and the sun

eats through the sheers. Here we are,
on a carpet with the world of toys splayed before us.

I'm reciting the alphabet, and your eyes

are wandering to the window where Stellar's Jays
are tearing at a squirrel's corpse in a tree branch.

There are things that you do not yet understand:

how Stellar's Jays look after each other—
which is a kind of love—that there can be song

in a city eating itself from the inside, that memory

is what remains to be said but it cannot be set
to the strings of an orchestra or passed

from one mouth to the next like a breath.

There is no space wider than that of grief,
there is no universe like that which bleeds.

May you never inhabit that universe. May you have

the world of toys. And may you hear, in these letters
I sing to you, the rustle of leaves and the possibility of opera,

softly over the tumult of everything.

Ghost Hunting as Physiography

The actors are green. They are on the dark side
of a water planet, and what they are doing is unholy.

The camera's night vision catches the glare of their eyes.
Alley-cat silent, they turn and hush each other

as if to say the ear is the beginning of the world. And
it is the faculty here that sets the breath back. Each person holds

a digital recorder, hoping to catch that beast voice . . .
that knuckled line of dialogue to drive up the ratings.

They are looking for a prologue to this new century
to start the heart—but nothing records, save

the singsong splinters of footstep
and the crunch of pulse in the throat. Wires stretch

into abyssal corridors, venous like the backs of the newly dead.
The building is a garden of odors: the fat funk of limestone, rust,

rodent piss, and damp, damp, damp. The camera's eye
sees the walls, glittered with sweat.

The first thermal image comes
from a crew member leaning on a wall. It is no ghost,

no signature of the past. Red and blue rings limn
the outline of a door. And through the door, nothing—

a room where a nurse hung herself from despair, where she appears
in midair like the moon in perigee. But not tonight.

Tonight, a shadow forms like fabric pulled from a roll.
The sound of a rubber ball slaps the tar of the rooftop

where tubercular children once played. And the boom mic
thuds against the hall joists as cast and crew sprint up the stairs .

Then the chill hook of an ice pick. Their breaths, like onion layers
unpeeling in the air and an orb glows before them like an oven.

It is metastatic. It shouldn't be but there it is. The eye knows it.
Then gone. A coin up the sleeve. Poof, our foundling belief

that the body is that which cannot be created or destroyed. It just is
and will ever be. The past is ruled by magnets. Imagine an apparition,

it will be. The lens does as it's told. And because the dead
are told to act their part, they perform like stand-ins,

rusty, holding scripts as the audience watches.
Memory is not instantaneous. The void is a distance

best traveled by car. And when the production wraps,
the husk of the hospital will stay risen and cooled.

The dead will go on, circling in their black laps, and the television
will flash and beam white noise from the other side.

Requiem

Where lie the open acre and all limns? Where the shade

    and what edges? What serrated blades and what cuts?

Where are we, leather-skinned, a spindle of nerves

    and frayed edges? What spare parts are we now

who have gone to the orchard and outlasted

    the sun and the good boots? The once tongued

salt from a tooth-cut wound scars now. The scars

    the deep-ruts of tree root where the earth's worn away.

And now, what? Salt? The memory of youth? The long

    hours of hands holding trembling hands? And what of the hard

breaths and the crack of a bullet against a trunk. Leave it

    to memory and memory's unmaking. Leave it

to the sun's hot sear and the haze-induced recollections. Leave it

    to the hours and the hours and the hours.

Eschatology in Five Acres

I'm concerned about the spotted mare
from the pasture, a boggy footpath away.
The decaying stumps and stumps of trees
thumb, as I walk to her, giants of another century.
But I am not in my body, and they are reveries
of a past life. Decades ago, possibly,
a barbed wire fence cut its meandering spine
through the five acres here to there,
a thorny trellis dividing what was ours
from what was the trillium's. And now
the cedar says otherwise.

Now the sweep of November winds
have felled a tree by its root ball,
snapping the barbed wire and freeing the mare
to wander into the service road. She's eating
by my rickety bird feeders but the sparrows don't mind
and neither does the totality of grass.
Crater by crater, she walks up the muddy slopes.
I think about her owner whose window I can see
from where I stand—the lights from the kitchen,
a modest planet or a star that's died
light years from here. I try to circle around her
with a saddle blanket, to calm her nerves,
and she lets me, but otherwise, her will is her will.
It is the last banquet before winter so I forgive her.

Yesterday in the paper the owner's son had died. Flatly,
the script told of a convoy and of a bomb
and how some sons lived and how precise
the journey is from a pasture to the phantom of a son.
It is like a moment when looking up from unloading
a bale of hay from the back of a pickup, you glance
and see a horse in some other field, porcelain in the sun.

The wire no longer possesses her, nor
the pasture, nor the horizon. The winds of November
can't lift the newsprint from the hands of a father
in a kitchen who's filled his mug with brandy
and coffee. And the mare who was never yours
is indifferent to you.

Self-Portrait as a Series of Non-Sequential Lessons

I cannot eat orange rinds, cannot
take all the Swedish Fish from the candy bins
just because they are jewels from a stony
country, that the aquarium glass is not

glad for my face, and there is often
deep water beneath the surface ice.
While driving cross-country, it is a good idea
to pack a lunch, else you get stared at

by old men with dirt on their caps and
steer manure on their boots when you go
for fast food, but it's nothing
serious, it's just common curiosity which is

normal with teenagers, particularly when
it comes to the opposite sex, like the time when
I watched the sky from the corner
doorway of a girl's house and I wanted to kiss her but

she moved away because she had someone
else in mind and didn't want to hurt me . . . because
I had a car and good taste in music
and because my adoration was an anchor

like a blackberry thorn on her dress.
When there are seismic events,
run under the door frame or hide
under a desk because when the world

calls like a mother to her appointed duties
she'll set you to some task, like food gathering
or wood piling, but it rains—often,
and those cannons they fire into the sky to cause storms

actually don't work . . . actually don't
do a damn thing except make a lot of goddamn noise
and the windows shake from the booms
because the house is old and I am getting older

and parts of me shake and will shake more, and I tremble
as I write this because the sun now has just
hid like a child behind a fish tank, and
the once shiny stones that had lined the bottom

are covered with moss, and the mossy hair
on your head keeps me awake at night and it is an odd
sort of worship that holds me here knowing
how little I know, how much I have to fear.

The Boy with the Fiddle in a Crowded Square

The young are so talented, my father says to me
as he palms a bill to drop into the boy's violin case.
Early, and the market is a riot with greens. Each stand
parades its wares while other parents cart by

with children in their strollers. My son is not listening
to the music—he's off somewhere in his dreaming mind
where anything can be hidden and people are ghosts.
I drop a dollar at the musician's feet, and he gives a light nod,

the market traffic weaving around us like luminous boats.
In my head, I'm writing a letter to my father, explaining
how every mistake I've made is palpable now,
the way the clouds take on human flaws with the wind.

I'm telling him the long fly balls I missed in little league
are dropping, one by one, at my feet. I'm penning
the collapse of each of my coliseums because right now,
son-hood is a promise of ruination and this violin song,

the hymn of its republic. Tonight, I will write a real letter
to my son. It will reveal footprints on each proving ground
and halve every distance I've traveled. The earthen line
of my pen will hum as my son's eyes read each line.

He will know each disappointment is a note like the wind
passing through the cable of a bridge. Each song
will rise, and hold the people in this market above
ragged waters. They will know how to listen. To parse

each other's hearts by bending forward as my father does now,
smiling at the fiddle player, then at my son. Slowly,
the soloist's notes thin into sliced apples—the crowd's
polite applause surging, then gone.

Colony Collapse Disorder in
Honey Bees as Eschatology

The alfalfa is heavy with providence. Chewed, the clover
grows back over the road as summer attempts a return.

White beehives jut in the field. Strange filing cabinets.
Little conundrums. The frames are pulled

and strewn here and there. They are like old countries,
ruins visible from the valleys below. I want to know

what makes their order so beautiful. The way they sleep.
The way you can walk through short cornrows with your palms out,

touch the blades, then stop and mark your place
with their separateness, their bleached wills.

The days are warm. All spring, pollen coats the acres.
Fine yellow dustings, the swizzle of rye.

Everything is a low hum. When it is time to move the boxes,
the world fundamentally changes. Such things transpire at night

but now it doesn't matter. For the cells are empty.
The colony, gone, and the boxes are pure allegory.

The hive bodies are a thousand hollow rooms—
pinhole crypts with their wax casings.

Minutes return like a drunken hand to the neck of a bottle.
There are no broods. At least at the destruction of Vesuvius,

there were remains: the hard carbonized body of a boy
holding a dog, food on the floor, the delicate touch

of two lovers twined in embrace. Here, silence.
The night bell sinks its teeth into a beekeeper's hand.

It is that moment when waiting becomes an act of holiness
and the flowers lock themselves in little *X*'s.

But night does not wait for the bees. It is like speaking to someone
you love in the dark who's fast asleep. The queen is gone

and the hive has left to find its own dance. Mist from the body
like smoke from a smudge pot. Then a small hole in a box

and absent hums spreading over the landscape like oil.

Prayer for What Won't Happen

I'll entrust that I'll keep on living for you—
that the knot in my throat is no longer there

to obscure us from whatever life might mean.
That really, it was an outcropping of stone

meant only to hold you here the way some marker
denotes distance or even time. Maybe,

in some galaxy we are admired for
our dangers and for the lives

we live despite ourselves. I believe this
as surely as the sound our rain gutters make

tonight in this unseasonable storm. That sound
so much like the light tap of a prayer block.

As sure as my pulse
I'm going to believe that this rain is not isolated,

that the two of us will keep
dreaming our animal dreams

and that every petty blasphemy I utter swirls
into the gutter in a green patina. Afraid? Yes.

What I fear should never be heard. It should be
quick as an eighth note or pressed down with steam.

Each night with you, I will hand over my stories
for another time. I will pick, from the ruins,

only that which I'm willing to carry. Only that
which I'll fail to replace. I am never leaving.

On the high hill overlooking our house, I'll make a clearing.
The moon will take up half the sky. It will hold you

without abandon, having neither love nor intent.

The Surgical Theater as Spirit Cabinet

I am without wings and obsessed with each patients'
        dark physics—the way their eyes are the copper bells
signaling the end of intermission.

It is here I come to peel away all guarantees.
        Gurneys line the hallway, some of them empty, some
with old men or children hooked to machines whose hum
        is something I can sleep against.

If this is what I'll become, then let me turn
        into a puff of smoke. Let me hide
in the warm lining of a pocket.

Somewhere behind me, men talk through
        their masks and as they speak I feel the space
between the air and my body. It is too bright,
        and the world becomes unknowable.

There is a chasm of indifferences as I am pushed
        to the double door. It's all so rehearsed.

Before my turn, I think about what I love
        the most and remember the audience, the man
whose wallet is found in his neighbor's bustier
        or the woman's watch now on the wrist of the magician.

I know. That's not love, but a sleight of hand.
        Presto, our lives bound from out of a top hat.

Now you see me and soon I'll be sawed in two.
        My brain sets its wavelengths on the flourish
of the sorcerer's cape.

                    The voice's redirection
and the sotto voce of the operating room's radio.
            There is nothing up their sleeves and

I am beginning to understand
            my body as the little curtain closes.

The magician's assistant disappears—slips
            through the trap door soundlessly—my own
thin voice the hollow slap of a hand on a cabinet.

By Subtraction

The wind shakes the chimes
into the siding, and the dog shakes too
though he doesn't wake you
as I carry you to the bedroom. Small mouth
sipping breath, you are fish-strange,
bejeweled in the dimness of the microwave's
nightlight. As I turn my back to the bulb
I make your form in my arms a dark weight
but you are no anchor. Together
we are sloops trailing a tiny wake in the carpet.
In the dark it's hard to navigate the furniture
so I count distance—five paces
from the tile to the sofa. From the sofa,
twelve to the hall. I'm subtracting
my steps to see what's left. The things
that burden me, like our lame dog's shattered nail,
blood on the carpet from his paces
to the food dish, our drafty house, all are outpaced.
There are no barriers, and I step over
the hound's dozing form as a quick gust cuts
dead branches from the pine and the drifts
lock our cars in. But I'm still counting—
the none-stars in the winter sky,
each hazily wrapped and strobing. The far bell
over the deep waters of your sleep. Two steps to the corner
where there are no animals nor animal danger. Two
to the bed where behind us the shadow of the dog
could be distant hills, where the clouds disassemble,
where your breaths pull the warmth of the room in
and where my face, my eyes are the glint of ore
from a country far away and known only in a language,
light as the syllables of exhalation.

Requiem

What then, of the orchards? What then

       of the tree limbs, dark and heavy with fruit? What of the stolen

pistol and the animal deaths suffered in the heavy sun? And what of

       our masks, the resonant pitch of our throats as we'd cry

fair or foul with each blow from a fist? What of the orchards

       where we grew long as the bramble and just as jagged?

Where our hearts kept pace with the sprinkler heads' *chk chk chk*?

       Where the gauzy horizon was like a belt cinched around

our waists, keeping us together despite our youth?

       What of our youth? What, then, of our youth?

Of the cheap indiscretions with a stolen flask,

       and a glance at skin magazines? Where we earned quick dollars

doing nothing except being boys, learning without comprehension,

       the difficult industry of men?

Self-Portrait with What Remains

What do I remember about the orchard?
                                          I feel it, mostly,
in my nose. My long whistling breath and night bouts

of emphysema. That I had a criminal disdain for the world
and for the work, which was shit, but gave me cash

to hold my solitude with newly bought cassettes.
And that I hated the safety of my town whose one strip mall

slipped by most drivers. I hated my youth
and sought the silence in rows of fruit trees

where I worked a good many summers. Sometimes, the orchard
wore insecticide in elegant yellow sashes—a bright

film on spider web lattices.
                                          What do I remember?
The quiet, mostly. Other boys arched over

like their own tombstones, and the white salt
on the brim of my ball cap. That after we reached our quotas,

we'd race back to the warehouse where the landowner
kept his modest livestock, and we'd beat

the penned up goats with switches broken
from apple branches. And in defiance, once,

hot-rodding in a tractor, we backed over a box of chicks
and what remained was a single wing without a body.

The thought of it still hurts me when I breathe. The wing there,
cropped as though the bird took off without it.

The bit of blood mashed into the tread and the unsteady laugh
of the other boys.
                    What do I remember? That I'm thirty-six . . .

that I'm a father and particular pitches of my infant son's squawks
mean hunger or sleep. That the yellow birds stitched on his plush toy block

are not ghosts and that not everything is a metaphor.
That the music on cassettes warp with age and that there's nothing

salvageable from time on that orchard except for a few words,
apparitions of tanned boys painting the bases of apple trees,

and a paraph of a broken image at near the end, where nothing is resolved.
It just is.
                    And this? This is what's left—my night coughs. Slips of news

clippings from the old town sent in the mail. The know-how
of tractor management. Now, where once resided

acrimony for youth's black seed—nothing except a single wing
opening and closing and opening again to catch the wind.

And what remains are my son's outstretched arms
wanting nothing more than to be held aloft.

Acknowledgments

Grateful acknowledgments to the readers and editors of the following publications where many of the poems in this book first appeared:

Chattahoochee Review—"Self-Portrait as a Small Town," "Self-Portrait Beside a Dead Chestnut Horse," and "Self-Portrait with What Remains."
Cimarron Review—"Self-Portrait with Taxidermy."
The Collagist—"Autumn Scene as Lullaby," "Autumn Song in Four Variations," "The Boy with the Fiddle in a Crowded Square," "In Defense of Small Towns," and "Self-Portrait as the Burning Plains of Eastern Oregon."
Crab Creek Review—"Eschatology on Interstate 84 at 70 mph" and "Eschatology through a Confluence of Trees."
Diode—"Insomnia as Transfiguration," "No One Sleeps through the Night," "Prayer for What Won't Happen," and "The Surgical Theater as Spirit Cabinet."
Guernica Magazine—each "Requiem" poem previously appeared as part of the long poem "Requiem for the Orchard."
Linebreak—"Self-Portrait Descending Slowly into the Atlantic Ocean."
MiPoesias—"Cussing in the Playground, "The Poet at Ten," and "Sticks and Stones."
The National Poetry Review—"Ablation as the Creation of Adam" and "How I Learned Quiet."
OCHO—"Self-Portrait in My Mother's Shoes."
Oranges & Sardines—"And When I Grew Up," At the Time of My Birth . . .," and "At the Time of My Young Adulthood."
Pistola—"If, Given" and "At the Time of My Death."
Puerto Del Sol—"Self-Portrait on Good Friday as an Altar Boy."
River Styx—"Self-Portrait with Schlitz, a Pickup, and the Snake River."
Sou'wester—"Colony Collapse Disorder in Honey Bees as Eschatology," "Ghost Hunting as Physiography," and "Television as Tool for Remission,"
The Southern Review—"Self-Portrait with a Spillway."

"By Subtraction" previously appeared in the West Coast Kundiman Chapbook, published by Achiote Press.

Thanks to the Artist Trust and to Western Washington University for financial assistance which greatly aided in the completion of this book.

Many thanks to the friends, family, and colleagues who made the time alone at the writing desk possible: my Kundiman posse, Jennifer Chang, Sarah Gambito, Joseph Legaspi, Vikas Menon, and the brilliant, brilliant fellows and faculty members. Thanks to Rick Barot, Bruce Beasley, Sandra Beasley, Jim Bertolino, Mary Biddinger, Anita Boyle, Stacey Lynn Brown, Nick Carbo, Elizabeth Colen, Marc Geisler, Rigoberto González, Carol Guess, Lee Gulyas, Kelly Magee, Adrian Matejka, Erika Meitner, Brenda Miller, Aimee Nezhukumatathil, Nancy Pagh, Suzanne Paola, Jon Pineda, Barbara Jane Reyes, Jay Robinson, Patrick Rosal, and Kathryn Trueblood. Many, many, many thanks to Martín Espada for selecting this book. And as ever, love to Meredith, Lucas, and my parents.

artist‖**TRUST**

SUPPORTING ART AT ITS SOURCE

Akron Series in Poetry
Mary Biddinger, Editor

Barry Seiler, *The Waters of Forgetting*
Raeburn Miller, *The Comma After Love:*
  Selected Poems of Raeburn Miller
William Greenway, *How the Dead Bury the Dead*
Jon Davis, *Scrimmage of Appetite*
Anita Feng, *Internal Strategies*
Susan Yuzna, *Her Slender Dress*
Raeburn Miller, *The Collected Poems of Raeburn Miller*
Clare Rossini, *Winter Morning with Crow*
Barry Seiler, *Black Leaf*
William Greenway, *Simmer Dim*
Jeanne E. Clark, *Ohio Blue Tips*
Beckian Fritz Goldberg, *Never Be the Horse*
Marlys West, *Notes for a Late-Blooming Martyr*
Dennis Hinrichsen, *Detail from* The Garden of Earthly Delights
Susan Yuzna, *Pale Bird, Spouting Fire*
John Minczeski, *Circle Routes*
Barry Seiler, *Frozen Falls*
Elton Glaser and William Greenway, eds.,
  I Have My Own Song for It: Modern Poems of Ohio
Melody Lacina, *Private Hunger*
George Bilgere, *The Good Kiss*
William Greenway, *Ascending Order*
Roger Mitchell, *Delicate Bait*
Lynn Powell, *The Zones of Paradise*
Dennis Hinrichsen, *Cage of Water*
Sharmila Voorakkara, *Fire Wheel*
Kurt Brown, Meg Kearney, Donna Reis, Estha Weiner, eds.,
  Blues for Bill: A Tribute to William Matthews
Vern Rutsala, *How We Spent Our Time*
Clare Rossini, *Lingo*
Beckian Fritz Goldberg, *The Book of Accident*